I Am Not Nitin

Nitin Srivastava

pencil

ISBN 978-93-5559-172-2

Published in India 2021 by Pencil

A brand of
One Point Six Technologies Pvt. Ltd.
123, Building J2, Shram Seva Premises,
Wadala Truck Terminal, Wadala (E)
Mumbai 400037, Maharashtra, INDIA
E connect@thepencilapp.com
W www.thepencilapp.com

Author biography

He is basically an engineer, working at the post of Asst. Professor at FGIET Raebareli India. He started writing as his hidden thirst, as he was interested in writing from the beginning but, not got the time before, because, he had decided to make a career in engineering. After achieving that career, he decided to fulfill his thirst and started writing. 'The God Factor – For Success and Contentment' was his first book. He has interest in writing on the topic of spirituality and motivation. Spirituality is always his basic quest. This book as well as the first book, is also concerned with spirituality.

Connect with [Nitin Srivastava]

I really appreciate you reading my book! Here are my social media coordinates:

Friend me on Facebook: @authornitinfans

1. Follow me on Twitter: http://twitter.com/nitinsri982

CONTENTS

The Quest 6

THE UTILITY 29

THE CURTAIN 50

THE BEYOND 61

Preface

A question, 'who am I?' has always bothered me. This always remained the real and the biggest quest. I love this question. And in search of the answer I am writing this book. Maybe some day or other I will receive the answer.

Excellent is the question. Excellent should be the answer.

But whatever be the answer, I am sure about one thing: I am not Nitin.

This is the search in this book. Those who identify with my quest will surely want to read this book, and I am hoping that by reading, they will find their search becomes more authentic.

So, this is not only my search but it is search of everyone.

The Quest

Once, Bodhidharma reached China. The King was waiting at the border to welcome him. He was a popular man. But, the King was surprised, "what type of man is this?"

Bodhidharma was wearing his shoes on his ears, as if they were not shoes but earrings.

The King was surprised.

He stood across a man who looked like a mad man - as if possessed by a ghost. Any normal person would be scared by his looks. But people love this man as a saint should be loved. Even the King was waiting to welcome him.

Bhodhidharma was a great saint and a very knowledgeable person. No one could compete with his qualities. He was incomparable. He was just like Buddha; nothing less than that, but, a furious looking man.

So the King started to think, he was mistaken to have recognized this man as the great Bodhidhama. May be this man is just a false saint. May be he was fooling. It was perfectly natural for the King to think this way - we all think like this, when we make an image of a person by just his physical appearance.

The King was also making this mistake of recognizing a person like Bodhidharma by the outer appearance. You cannot recognize a mystic by his outer appearances.

So, the King was confused. But he was waiting and had waited so long.

But, now he grew confused about asking his question at all.

A tension had arisen in his mind. He was hopeful of getting the answer, but his tension consumed him. Tension in front of Bodhidharma was natural, because no explanation could be given about this man - he was inimitable.

The King asked himself, "what if I don't get an answer? I have suffered. Therefore, would I have wasted all that time?"

So, he welcomed Bodhidharma.

After all how could he judge a person like Bodhidharma, without asking anything?

But Bodhidharma had made a long journey. So, the King also had to take him to the guest house. The King asked Bodhidharma to come with him. After reaching the palace and before wishing him a good night's rest, the King asked his question very eagerly, "I am a King, and I don't understand but because of one reason or another, I am always anxious and restless. Please help."

Bodhidharma said, "Okay! You come to me at 4 o' clocks in the morning with your anxiety and restlessness. Show me these things and I will throw them away."

The King was a little surprised, "Tension or restlessness are not of the material world. So how can I show them? This man must be mad." The King departed wishing him good night.

After dinner the King went to the bedroom. But he remained restless; this so called Saint made him more restless. He never experienced this overwhelming restlessness; never in his life. He tried to sleep but sleep was far away. And nobody could sleep after seeing such a furious face of Bodhidharma. He remained puzzled the whole night.

But now it was 4 o' clock in the morning and he decided to go ahead and see what Bodhidharma response would be, after all, he had waited so long for this moment.

When he reached the guest house, he saw a huge crowd of disciples, amidst whom Bodhidharma was sitting. Seeing the crowd it became more difficult for the King to ask his question and receive an answer. He hesitated as he draws near Bodhidharma, who was watching him.

Suddenly, Bodhidharma spoke, "I was not expecting you alone! Where are the others who were bothering you so much?"

Now, it became more difficult for the King to understand.

He was hesitant to say anything. Feeling helpless he said, "I am here, now please guide me."

Bodhidharma asked him to sit down with closed eyes and search, for his tension and restlessness. And Bodhidharma said, "When found tell me and I will solve your problem. I will throw these things away."

The King followed the instructions.

Sitting down with closed eyes, he passed two hours in meditation.

Bodhidharma asked him, "Now stop! Enough is enough. Have you found what are you searching for?"

The King answered, "No! But, now there is no need. I understand what you wanted to say. And to my surprise I have never felt such a peace within."

The King thanked him and departed for the palace.

The King had searched his tensions as if they were some material object inside of him and found nothing. Try this meditation.

……………..*************……

…………

Now I proceed further.

For this was the beginning of great understanding by the King, whomever he thought he was, might not be that person. He might be quite different. He was thinking himself a King, realized then and there he had been playing a role given by society, and he had to search for his real identity.

And we all have to search for our real identity.

Until now I was thinking myself as Nitin, which is my given name, but, is this really my real identity? Or does there is another identity beyond this name.

So, I decided to go deep into this quest, even though I perceived that this quest is not that easy to answer.

The story begins at my birth; when a nameless squirmy creature had been born. Everybody had born nameless.

So, fortunately or unfortunately, I have taken birth on this rare planet earth. I was nameless so far.

When somebody is born on this earth, he or she must be given a name. A name not only represents a tag for recognition but it represents hope; hope of parents; hope of society. A name is just not a name, it is much more.

So, I was born; a hope was born.

When a child is born in a family, how precious is that new born baby for the entire family? He or she is the center of attention. The family perceives a new ray of light, into his or her eyes; the ray of hope, that this child is going to open new horizons.

A child is a new born future for the family; a telescope, through which the future is standing clear and near to their eyes.

A society can do nothing but give a name to this newborn person, so that, to give everyone the ability to know who this person is.

This name by and by becomes this person's identity, to such an extent that anyone cannot recognize him or herself without this name.

But for me this remained the real quest. Who am I?

Could this name really my identity or I am someone else also?

Suppose I was born in place of Albert Einstein exactly at same time and place when Einstein born and from the parents of Albert Einstein. Then what do you think what name would I have?

In that case you can guess my name............

Or, suppose I was born in place of Mahatma Gandhi exactly at same time, place and parents. Then what would my name be?

I think this time also you can guess................

Or, suppose I was born in place of Hitler. Now also you can guess my name........

I could have more than billions of names by just replacement of time place and parents to which I am born to.

Our birth is just accidental.

The name with which I identify much saying I am so and so and I belong to such a family is just accidental.

So, I was born nameless but as a hope for my family. Someday this child could possibly raise the name of the family by becoming successful. I think every father and mother in this world asks this question to their child, "What will you become; A doctor or engineer, someone big."

The question shows the longing of parents for their child to achieve something in the society.

And the name is just not a name; it is also a projection of this longing, this desire.

In India some of the families have a tradition of giving name to the child ceremonially, and the ceremony is named as, 'naam karan sanskar'. The ceremony includes giving name to the child by some senior respected member of the family or by some priest and after that a big party is arranged; the name is celebrated. But, what is the purpose of making such a fuss for just a name?

After all a name is a name - a device to recognize a person, that should be all. But in our society a name is not an ordinary device to recognize, it is more than that; it is the cause of the image or ego which is attached to this name. And society is making every effort that you become this name, you become so close to this name that it becomes impossible for you to think your self-image is nothing else than a name - you are unable to think that you could be beyond this name. The society is not interested in your feeling. The society is interested in making you more your name, than a person.

The society is interested in forming you into a person like the King, not a saint like Bodhidharma. Because Bodhidharma is so ordinary that he could wear his shoes in place of earrings, the King is specific. A king can be utilized for welfare of the society, he can generate great kingdoms, but a Bodhidharma is not at all interested in any kingdom. He is happy in any situation.

Society wants you to be specific, so that you can perform some specific task for it.

That is why an ego or image is generated around your name. And the ego and the attachment are so great that you can even fight for your name. Look at it - a foolish man abuses you and you start fighting back without realizing his foolish attitude. Is this not your ego in action?

Man lives for his name, as if name is everything in his life.

We might take leave from our work and visit a hill station or other tourist sites to revive our passion and celebrate some days' rest. But why do we need to go to the places far away from where we live? Why can't we find rest at our own home? What is the purpose of going to a distant place?

And you feel good when visiting such places, sometimes an awesome experience. Perhaps you are in heaven. Being away from your routine life and you might feel exceptionally good.

But, what is the reason? Why do you feel so good?

Try to observe this. Also, attempt to search for the reason.

For myself, I had the opportunity to visit Shimla, a beautiful hill station of India, sent by my company for a working vacation. I was enchanted by the beauty of this lovely city. I met the friend whom I was scheduled to meet for business; a very nice guy, good looking and charming by nature. He welcomed me, "Good morning sir, and how you are and how was your journey?"

I said, "Oh! Yes I am fine my good friend, how are you? But, your city is like heaven, very beautiful."

He said, "Shall we proceed to the office?"

So, we then departed for the office, where we spent three hours, busily discussing the issues that were the purpose of my trip. Completing the official work, he invited me for lunch at the same hotel in which I stayed for the night after which I had to return.

So, we arrived at the hotel. While eating lunch we discussed many things, including our personal lives etc. He had been a stranger when we met, but now we were acquainted to the point that he became almost like a close friend of mine. We were enjoying the lunch and the discussion between us. And at this point when we have completed the official work and I had the whole evening free, I asked him, if he could make some arrangements so that I could see the beauty of Shimla. He readily accepted my request and told me that he himself would go with me to show the city.

After lunch, and taking a short rest I was ready for the local travel of Shimla along with my new friend. I so looked forward to a tour because, this was my first journey to any hill station and Shimla was really beautiful.

We hired a car from my hotel and decided to go to as many locations as possible in 3 - 4 hours. We travelled to selected locations, where we stopped for some time, to take some pictures and proceed to the next location.

I was enjoying myself; for me it was a great experience. Finally after visiting our destinations, we returned to the dining room of the hotel, where I ordered the dinner.

I was mesmerized with the beauty of Shimla. So, I spoke highly about the places we had visited. But, finally out of curiosity, I asked him, "What do you feel about this city. I think you are very lucky, that you are living in such a beautiful place."

But, I was surprised by his answer.

He said, "Do you really want to know how I feel?"

I said, "Yes I want to know how you lucky people feel about living in this city."

He said, "This city is a boring place."

I said with surprise, "What? What are you saying? I would never expect that answer."

He explained further, "Yes! For me this is a boring place. You are thrilled to see a hill station for the first time as a guest. But, ask the residents here, seeing daily the same trees, same rocks, same clouds and not even that, life is difficult here - a struggle for water, for electricity etc. So, for me life here is boring."

The answer was very surprising for me.

We had spent a lot of time together and now it was the time to say good bye. He was a nice man, honest also, because he accepted the fact that even Shimla is not any different or unique place. It's your own perception that makes it special or ordinary.

But what is the reason, why do we feel good while visiting such places?

Why did my new friend say such a beautiful place was boring? At that time, I didn't have an answer. But after that experience, I was motivated to get the answer.

…………….*******************…

…..……

'Identification', is the reason. Because, my friend belonged to Shimla, he had been living there so long; he got identified with that place.

Try to understand this. You visit a new place which you have never seen or, maybe you vacation there a weak. You feel good. What is happening there to your being?

You lose identity with yourself; not fully, but at least to some extent. You don't see the things you usually see, you don't see or meet people you usually see or meet. This helps you drop your identification with your home city or the place you belong to. And, the new scene helps you drop tension and stresses, related to the society you belong to.

This drop of identification, with your body, with your mind, gives you some pleasure. Your attention shifts from your body, to the new objects or people.

Take another example:

Have you loved someone?

Love is the most beautiful thing in this world. Nothing can be more beautiful. Have you been in love for even a single moment in your life? How was the feeling? Can you remember, or can you feel? You must have felt great. No other feeling is parallel to the feeling of love. Earth is revolving around sun as if she is in deep love.

Love is the cause. Nothing less than love can satisfy you; as Jesus said, "God is love".

I remember:

My love, my first love, who is luckily my wife now - I remember the day when I saw her photograph for the first time. In India most of the marriages are arranged, love marriages are rare. It isn't that I didn't come in contact with other girls, but I wasn't much interested in girls, as a good career was my only goal. But after getting the right job, getting confident enough that I could now afford a marriage, I decided finally, to marry. For the purpose, I gave an advertisement in a newspaper, so the right person could approach us.

So many photographs were sent to me, but on seeing that particular photo, I was so pleased and felt a great love, which I had never felt for any other girl; I would say it was love even before first sight because till that time I had not even seen the girl. From that photograph, my journey of love life started and for the first time, I felt the bliss which I never felt before.

The photograph was of a simple girl, without much makeup, but beautiful.

What can be said about love? It happens, and when it happens, nothing can be done. Sometimes, I listen to people, say, "love your work, love your brother, and love your village, love this and that." But, I am sorry, love cannot be forced. It happens, helplessly, and you cannot do anything about this. You become helpless and that is the sign of love. You fall away, as if only the other exist, you don't.

And that was happening with me. Only one photograph existed; I was in love with the photograph. Whenever I got the chance, I tried to see the photo.

Now, my father and the family were busy in choosing from the photos, which of the girls I should meet at first. But my emphasis was wholly on how to meet the girl I had chosen or, you can say I was in love with! So, every time I was asked, I took her photo and tried to convince that she and her family seemed to be the best.

I am telling you my arranged love story. That may seem a joke to you but that is true.

So, finally we all decided a date to meet her and her family. I was really excited or you could say most excited, I had taken half day leave for the purpose, of trying to be ready as best as possible, for me. Because, I was not that handsome-guy; so, there was also the possibility of my rejection, though I tried my best.

Reaching her house and feeling both - excited and nervous, I met her parents and brother who greeted us first. We entered the house, in the drawing room and sat on the seats offered. Formal talking was going between us, but, inside I was waiting, only to meet my girl whom I had started loving; by just seeing her photo.

And, that is why I was so nervous. Love always makes you nervous, but, that nervousness is also beautiful. I was nervous, because of the shift of attention from myself, to the other, whom I started loving; now the center of your attention is my lover not me.

That is love, 'You feel nervous, because now you want to impress him or her. You feel nervous because now you want to see a fulfillment in his or her eyes. But, that very nervousness fills you with bliss'.

Love is bliss in itself. It shifts your attention, from yours to the other you love. You lose your identity to some extent. And this loss of identity with your body, with your thoughts makes the experience of love a blissful experience. Try to understand this.

I was nervous because, I was going to meet, to see my love for the first time. Everybody was busy talking, but, my eyes were searching for my love. Finally she appeared in a yellow sari – a good looking girl, 5'5", a good height, with sharp features; she was looking gorgeous.

She came and sat in front of us, after wishing Namaste, to all of us. In India the meeting like this is quite similar to a job interview, as if a girl is going to attend an interview for a job and her whole life depends on this. So, normally this type of meetings is tension for the girls also.

But, I was looking at her as if I had been waiting for her, for many years. Love is always like that. I have felt the nervousness she was going through. So, I have decided not to talk to her at that time and in this manner tried to reduce her tensions. This was my first acquaintance of her and for me that was enough. More than enough! Because, when you love somebody, everything else other than love, becomes worthless.

Love is like the flowering of a rose. A rose in flowering doesn't know who you are, a sinner, or a saint. Whomsoever you are, it is going to grip you with its fragrance.

That is why talking to her and trying to know about her history or nature or idols etc. seemed useless affair to me. I was mentally prepared to accept this proposal of marriage.

Love is like this. If you start loving a person then you can never think about his or her characteristics; you cannot. You are helpless; you just love, that is all.

So, we said nothing in that meeting. But everybody else was talking with each other. After, talks with tea and snacks, we decided to depart, and promised to answer after a little bit of discussion at home.

That is how marriages are generally fixed in India.

So, we reached home and every one of us is quite satisfied and as far as I was concerned, I was more than ready.

So, next day we gave our positive answer. And the answer was yes from that side also. So the marriage was fixed. The date of marriage was decided later on, with the consent of both sides and for that we had to wait for six months. So, I and my girl had six months' time, to be in romance without marriage.

Really, those days were most beautiful days in our life. Got the approval for marriage and hence freedom for dates or talks.

That was an approval for me to talk with my beloved; at least on the phone. The phone was a comfortable medium, because it was not always possible to meet. I was doing my job and she was also busy at home. There were many other reasons we could not make a date. It was an arranged marriage we needed over time to develop trust. That was the reason mobile phones could do the best job.

But, it took me approximately a week's time before I was able to make my first call. I was hesitating to call her because; I didn't know her interest and nature.

Finally, I made a call. Her mother picked up the phone.

"Hello! I am Nitin! How are you?" I said

"Fine! How are you?" she asked

I said, "Very fine"

"You want to talk to Akanksha?" She replied.

And from here, a new journey started, of love, of romance, of togetherness, of fear, of courage…………………

If love is real, it includes all, every emotion. But love is bigger than all those emotions.

Her mother delivered phone to Akanksha.

For the first time I listened to her honey dipped voice.

Her voice was as beautiful as her looks.

"Hellooo! Wow, it is you. I am so happy!" she said

She must be happy finally, that, at least I had called her; after a long gap. A girl of this twenty first century cannot bear such a long gap. She must be thinking about me that this guy is definitely a shy person otherwise what was preventing him from talking before?

Anyways, I said, "Oh! Hi, how are you?"

"I am also happy that I am talking to you." I replied

But, it was not only a matter of talking seriously. When you are in love your whole personality speaks by itself; your voice, your way of talking, every aspect of your personality become a sign of love. Obviously, our love was also reflecting. Love is the most beautiful experience in this world. It seems to be coming from a different world, which is unknown but beautiful. Love always remains unknown. The more you feel you know it, the more unknown it becomes. We were passing through that experience, called love.

I was ecstatic, because I was thinking of her all the time and she was thinking of me all the time. No other thought remained. My mind was full of her and her mind was full of me. No space remained for tensions, for worries.

"I was thinking only of you" she replied

The voice was showing her love, her joy.

"Really!" I replied

I was very happy with her answer.

"Why have you taken so much of a time, calling me?" She asked.

"Oh! Nothing, I was somewhat hesitating. That is all." I said.

"Hesitating, For what? What are you saying? I started thinking that I was going to marry a very traditional typical Indian boy, who is too shy to talk with girls." she said with some complaint.

"I am sorry, but, I was just not able to judge, whether you would like it or not." I said

"Okay! Forget it, how are you now?" she said.

"I am fine." I said

Whatever we said to each other was immaterial; talking with her made me feel blissful. That was the beginning, of the experience of love. After that first talk, we started talking daily approximately eighteen hours a day. The experience was fabulous. And, those days were to remain unforgettable for the rest of our life. I cannot go into the whole talk between us; because I could write two or three novels on that. But, I described it only to make you understand that the experience of love is great and beautiful.

During that period, before marriage we talked so much, as if every moment of our life was for talk. There was no other source, so that we can remain in touch twenty four hours. And we wanted to remain in touch forever; this is also the feeling up until now, after six years of marriage.

Love gives you freedom. If it is real it gives you freedom. It is not bondage, as most of the people make it out to be. On the contrary, it is freedom.

And, when I say freedom, I mean love frees you from your thoughts; from your thoughts that you are this body and mind.

But, how it frees you from your body and mind is the question.

Gurdjieff said, “Identification is the only sin."

All your sorrow, your problems arise because, you identify yourself as your body or your mind. And, anything which shifts your attention from your body and mind gives you pleasure; fills you with delight, fills you with bliss.

Anything like love, or perhaps a journey to other place, may be a hill station or some beautiful resort, break this identification of yours with your body or mind, at least to some extent, and you start feeling blissful.

Try to understand this. Your identification that you are body or mind gives you a distorted perception of all the sorrows you have.

But, where this perception of identification that you have with this body or mind comes from, is a question. That is the quest we will try to solve.

Try to understand this.

When I was born, I was born nameless. Society had to give me a name. To recognize me or to separate me from the mob seemed the only purpose. But possibly there is also a hidden purpose to this name.

What game has society played with me? As I grew up, I grew up with this name. Society started calling me by this name. It called me by this name, so many times, that I started recognizing myself as this name 'Nitin'. I have forgotten completely that there may be some other identity of myself, because, I remain the same person whether I was called by this name or another.

I am not blaming the society. It has no other option. But, in this manner you start recognizing yourself as your name, as your body and as your mind. You get hypnotized and forgotten the fact that you are beyond all this, that you are or may be something different. You have gone through millions of births, through millions of names, but none of those names is with you now.

So, you have to go for the quest. If you stick to your name you forget the real quest and you get mixed up with this false illusive world which your name, your body has given to you.

Have you seen a robot? How it functions? How it understands?

To get a robot to work correctly, you have to make a proper communication with it, so that it can understand what function you want to perform with its help.

This purpose of communication is done with a program. A program is a set of commands, which make the robot understand what it has to do. For example, if you want the robot to wash your clothes, you have to make it understand, with the help of appropriate program, or if you want the robot to make tea for you, then you have to provide a program that can make a robot understand the methodology of making tea and then it can perform.

But, what is a robot?

It is a utility for you. That is why you need to train the robot or program the robot for your purpose.

In similar fashion you are a utility for the society. You have to serve some purpose or another for the society. Some of you have to become engineers, some others serve as doctors. Everybody is going to serve in some manner or the other.

And for your purpose society has to train you. And, robots can be trained without giving them any name. Only a program will serve the purpose.

But, to train a human, identification with his or her body and mind must be imposed. A person must be made to have the name for his or her body. Remember, you can only provide a name to the body not to the soul, or what lies beyond personal identification.

A name is to be provided and then by repetition identification is to be created.

I was given the name 'Nitin'. Then, through repetition of this name by the people surrounding me made me identified with this name and I became 'Nitin' for myself.

Now society could program me for the discipline it wants from me. Now society could make me serve some purpose for society.

But, this is a deep question, and because I am a rebel from the beginning. Only a rebel can ask this question. What is my existence beyond the society, beyond the name? Can society give me the answer about who am I, actually?

No! Not at all! No society can solve this question for me; because, this question is associated with my own self, and not related with the society.

A solution to this question can only be given to me by myself alone, not by the society. For the answer I have to go beyond this programming. Only then can I obtain my answer.

So, this is the real quest: who am I?

But, I am sure that I am not Nitin.

I cannot be so small that society can define me by a name.

I am not Nitin.

Thanks to God.

I am not Nitin.

………………ψψψψψ………………

THE UTILITY

Society wants to utilize you, for a purpose. Society is not the culprit, but, it has no option. All its affairs depend on how efficiently it utilizes you.

Society runs under a system, so that all the affairs go smoothly. It is a society which is running hospitals, it is a society which is running schools, it is a society which is doing all to make your life comfortable. You cannot escape from the society. Therefore, willingly or unwillingly you have to devote part of your life to the society.

So, society utilizes your body, your mind, anything you can offer to the society. And, your society has to program you, for one purpose or the other. If you have the potential to become a doctor, the society will provide you a medical training, or if you have potential to become an engineer, society will train you for that or some other training.

And, you by and by become attuned to the training. You start thinking yourself as somebody. You start identifying yourself with that very identification given by the society.

But, is that your real identity? Have you ever thought of that? I have closed my eyes many times and tried to find that Nitin, tried to find in which part of my body this Nitin could exist. But I find him nowhere. For society my body could be Nitin, but for me, I have not found him.

Society is very much interested in giving you identification, some sort of identification. But, is that your real goal to thoroughly accept this identification?

Society is dangerously interested; Okay! It is necessary, without it society cannot survive. But it is a dangerous interest.

One day I visited the house of one of my colleagues - a nice man with a beautiful family. He had two kids - both boys, one seven years old and the other four years old.

The elder child was named Rahul and the younger one was named Raj.

When I reached their home, the kids were playing hide and seek. I was welcomed by the colleague and his wife and offered a chair in the drawing room - I sat there waiting. They were gone for some time leaving me alone.

I was alone there looking over the decor of their drawing room, beautifully decorated with paintings and some show pieces.

Suddenly both boys came on playing joyfully, running after one another.

Even I was enjoying their play and the innocence of their play.

Children having fun is beautiful to watch. And, I was enjoying watching them.

A butterfly entered the room.

Rahul watched first and rushed to catch it.

I love that innocent smile on his face which he developed after discovering that butterfly; as if he found a treasure. We grownups don't always understand the child's ecstatic happiness, because, even real diamonds don't make us as happy as a butterfly can do for them. He was jumping in excitement.

"Raj! catch it, catch it." shouted Rahul

"Dada (elder brother)! What is this? How is it flying? Can I also fly like this?" Raj asked and started chasing the sorry creature.

I was viewing this whole thinking about the small creature with sympathy, but enjoying the joyous activities going around.

Suddenly, and fired by so many questions, made Rahul, somewhat angry over Raj.

"Don't ask so many questions, you fool! First catch the butterfly otherwise it will go away and we will not be able to catch it." Rahul voiced with anger.

So, both of them started chasing.

After ten minutes, activities continued. They were jumping from one sofa to another. I was sitting, but, they hardly noticed. Their faces were glowing with joy as people get in the presence of God. Their voices were as rhythmic as ringing bells of a temple.

I was watching with sheer pleasure; sheer because I felt the intensity of thrill in their beings and it carried over to me.

Their noise however was annoying their parents.

Their mother warned them to stop those annoying activities.

What is a disturbance, for one person could be pleasure for another depending on your attitude. However disturbing for their parents, I was still enjoying myself.

In the middle of all these activities and to make them happier another butterfly entered the room which was looking different from the earlier one, as God painted it with other colors.

Raj asked again, “Dada! Why this butterfly is looking different from that one."

Angered by the question, Rahul ordered, "Just concentrate on that butterfly and catch it and don't ask me the stupid questions."

The play continued another ten minutes.

Their play ended when both butterflies escaped from the window.

So annoyed, their mother gave last warning to them, "You children are hopeless. I am coming, and then I will see both of you."

But, they both enjoyed themselves to the fullest.

No parental warning was going to stop them.

After, much play Raj seated himself beside me and a series of questions started; now the target of questions was not Rahul, but me.

And, I was thinking as if seated on the hot seat of KBC; even sitting at KBC was not so difficult.

I had no option.

"Have you seen those butterflies?" asked Raj.

“Oh! Yes, I have seen." I answered.

"They were beautiful. Weren't they?" and again, next question.

"They were very beautiful, like you both." I tried to express my feeling for them both.

"How do they fly?" Raj, asked.

"They have wings, which help them get aloft and fly." I tried to explain.

But, my explanation was not to be understood by children of this age.

So, he again asked, "With the help of wings? But, why don't I have wings?"

Children are much more intelligent than their elders on some points. Even Einstein might not be able to answer their questions.

I was puzzled as how to qualify this bigger than KBC (A quiz program in India, where millions of Rupees can be won) quiz.

I actually didn't have the answer. Many Darwinian answers could be given but they were not going to satisfy the child's curiosity.

Before proceeding further into the incident I want to make it clear that why am I discussing this event. I want to emphasize how curious and intelligent children naturally are and how we as a society kill that intelligence, just to make them a better utility for the society. This is because being a utility pays, and playing time in solving curiosity pays nothing. This incident in itself reflects the utility oriented attitude of the society. An example is how my anecdote explains this incident.

Just it was difficult for me to give an answer, it was also difficult for him to understand. But, his curiosity was as intelligent as it was where Newton saw the apple falling off the tree.

"Well, God has given it the wings but not you." I answered.

"But why?" he asked

Now, it was more difficult for me to explain. So, I remained silent, just looking at him helplessly.

I was thinking about an explanation, but before I said something, he fired the next question.

"If I have wings, would it be possible for me to fly?"

Now, I couldn't give him some philosophical explanation. So, I gave the straight forward answer.

"No! Even with wings you cannot fly."

Unsatisfied by my answer, he asked, another question.

"If birds can fly on wings, then, why cannot I?"

"Because your weight is more and birds have lower weight due to hollow bones, which makes it easier for them to fly." I answered

Question and answer session between us were going on, when his parents entered the room. They apologized to me for the delay, saying how busy they were in something that couldn't be delayed.

I took a breath of relief, as the children would now be done quizzing me.

After apologizing and sitting on front sofa, Raj's mother scolded him and asked him to behave properly. Had he bothered me too much?

I'd already spent half an hour in that house and I planned to stay only a few more minutes. I want only other half an hour to be there not more. So, I told them that now I wanted to leave. But they told me, that they would not let me go without at least a cup of tea and some snacks.

During tea I and my colleague talked about some current political strategies of the government, as males often talk, men love the topic of politics and discussing the issues.

But, Raj's mother wanted to show her child's talent to impress me; how smart her son was in the studies. In some of the families I have seen this habit of showing their child's smartness or talent in front of friends, colleagues, neighbors etc.

Or, they also test their child in front of others thinking that may be in this manner they could make their child a good performer and a sincere student. They want to increase their child's sincerity.

Before their parents entered the room children were enjoying themselves. Now they were sitting silently as if any time they could be scolded. They sat stiffly as if they were going to enter an examination center. I even started to think that it was my fault that, coming to their home, I caused these kids to enter a quiz contest.

I was thinking that a KBC is going to start in that room and this time Rahul and Raj were the contestants and their parents are on Amitabh's seat. And, I was the spectator.

So, mother fired the first question to Raj.

"Raj! Tell me the spelling of apple."

"A P P L E" told Raj.

"Very good." his mother, praised.

Then looking at me his mother told me.

"I tell you sir, this guy is brilliant. He is very good at studies. He always scores number one in his class."

I nodded my head, in agreement. What else I could do and who is going to ask me for my opinion.

Again a series of questions was started and after every answer the parents didn't forget to show me that their kids were so brilliant.

This all ended, when I left their home, saying, good bye to them.

…………………..**************………
…….

Afterwards, I was thinking up a reason parents behaved like this? What was the need?

The reason is the foolish competition going on in the society, which is more interested in making man a utility than a person; the society is more interested in making man an object than a person.

This whole exercise the parents were doing, if you deeply observe, is actually an effort to make their children more valuable as a utility to society, so that in future they can earn a job and a paycheck. The more society can utilize them the more society will pay them in terms of money, in terms of respect, and so on.

Hence, the parents are giving every possible effort to make utilities from children. Even in front of guest or strangers their efforts continue, without any gap. I find this effort leaves little room for caring.

And, remember an object or utility is dead. An object cannot love; man can, a person can. A utility cannot love;

man can, a person can. An object cannot be happy; a man can, a person can.

In my opinion, the approach to child-reaming should be different. Emphasis should be given to develop feelings, not to become a utility.

The title of my book is named 'I am not Nitin'. But this is relevant also. In the previous chapter I explained that society has not given you the name just to recognize you, but, society is very smart because it can only program you to be used as a utility through a tool and that tool is your name. Without your name it cannot program you.

Robots can be programmed without a name. They don't have parents or teachers telling them their name and what job they would be good for. Just feed the required set of instruction to robot a, robot B or robot C and they will do the same job as the program or set of instruction says. But, to program a human or make a human fit for society, first a name is to be given and then the person should be called by that name so many times that the person start recognizing himself or herself with that name.

I was born nameless. We were all having born nameless. Society is helpless; it has to give you a name to recognize you. By and by your name moves so close to you that you become identified with it; as I become identified with Nitin. I started thinking myself as Nitin.

Everyone becomes identified with his name and surely doesn't recall anymore that the parents were responsible for that name.

In contrast robot is making to work as you wish through a set of instructions known as program. Humans cannot be controlled like this. Humans are to be programmed slowly, through conditioning or you could say hypnosis. Hypnosis is nothing but a pattern of repetition.

If certain thing is repeated in front of you several times then it forms a set pattern inside you and affects your behavior.

For example, have you ever thought about going to the market and why you purchase certain things over others or why advertising is so important for selling products? Because an advertisement not only makes you acquainted with the product but also should you experience repetition of that advertisement several times, you become hypnotized about the product and when you reach market you buy it.

Your name helps society to hypnotize you, to give you a set pattern. This pattern is your daily schedule, with little free time.

We have to understand this that is how a human is programed.

And we also have to understand that every human living in this world has two names. One name to be recognized by society and the other to be recognized by him or herself.

To understand this let us take an example. I'll take the example of myself. Society recognizes me by my name, 'Nitin'. But, how am I talking about myself? When I talk about myself I use the word 'I'. Hence, the word 'I' is the tool for me when I am talking about myself. Therefore, this word 'I' is my second name, which I use for myself.

So, every human is programmed by two sources - one is society and the other is he or she, himself or herself. These are the two sources of hypnosis.

Now, we have to understand more, how this hypnosis works?

For example, when I grew up as a child I was programmed that I was Nitin. I started identifying myself as Nitin. Further I was told that I or Nitin is a Hindu, so, I had to go to Hindu temples. So, I started recognizing myself as Hindu. But the question is being human is my real identity I realized just by place of birth I became a Hindu, my parents were Hindu, most around me were Hindu. Which identity is important? That means, when being Hindu if I feel superior, then, I am hypnotized because every human is of same status whether Hindu or not.

So, this was an example, to illustrate the process of programming or hypnosis by society. Similarly giving instructions to yourself also hypnotizes you. In this manner your whole personality as you are, depends upon two sets of instructions given to you - one is given by society and other given by you.

And don't think you don't treat yourself as a utility. You often treat yourself as a utility many times. Look into your life and you will find many events, many moments in which you are treating yourself as utility. You can recognize those moments - try to observe, you must be harsh, non-loving towards yourself in those moments.

When you target big and give yourself instructions to achieve that, what are you doing? You are playing the same game as society plays with you. You are making yourself a utility. I am not trying to restrict your dreams, but I'm encouraging you to determine whether you are harsh or loving towards yourself while you are fulfilling yourself.

Because, remember, a utility can never remain happy. A person can be blissful not a utility. Your name helps society to make you a utility. But, society doesn't have any option; it has to give you a name, it has to utilize you. But, you have the option. If you can remain aware of the fact that your name is not your real identity; if you can remain aware that your body is not your real identity; if you can remain aware that your mind is not your real identity, then bliss will enter your life.

And, that bliss is because, now you can be at least, somewhat close to your real identity; this is the real search of every human, whether this search is hidden or open, it is the real search.

You can observe, whenever you feel pleasure in life, at that time you becomes nobody without any ego, without any name. You are just present in the event, and out of your full consciousness. Remember yourself dancing. At the time you dance, do you remember your name or you just enjoy dancing. Definitely, you enjoy dancing.

When you are dancing, you are yourself, a person, doing as you wish for your pleasure, you are not being utilized. You remain a person, not a utility while dancing and that is why pleasure follows.

Pleasure can follow a person, but not a utility. I have seen many people saying that they are doing many good deeds, much good for society but then also their life is miserable; not happy. They cannot remain happy. They are committing a basic mistake. Perhaps they forget people can do good things and not be a utility.

Their focus is towards becoming a utility all the while becoming happy or feeling generous. Their goodness is making them an object not a person. They could remain happy if somehow they could withdraw their ego from their good deeds but often they can't.

And, the ego is given by identification; identification with name, with body or mind. Dropping identification with name, body and mind makes you a person because it drops the programming given to you.

So, search for your real identity. Become a person not an object.

Then pleasure will follow you. Just like in dance where you forget your identity.

It is like

Dance is within you.

You are the dance.

But, how can you dance, when you are identified with your broken leg.

You, becoming your name, is identifying, with a broken leg.

Your name is your society entering you.

Your name is your broken leg.

Pleasure can enter your life, with courage.

Courage to dance;

Dance with your other leg.

Real identification is your healthy leg.

You can dance over that.

Your being is your real identity.

Dance, with your being, with your real identity is possible, when you drop your false identity.

'The pleasure happens.'

..................**************.........

....

I have an anecdote to tell:

I read this anecdote, when I was a teen ager. This influenced me and my life very positively. I really don't remember, the person, from whose life I am taking this incident, but, he was a well- known doctor. I will call him Dr. Barnard.

So, following is the anecdote:

"I was walking towards my chamber in some hurry, through the corridor of the hospital, when a boy, of nearly thirteen years of age collided with me in his wheel chair." Dr. Barnard was writing, while describing an incident.

Dr. Barnard was a well-known heart surgeon in his country. And, he also was known as a well-known writer. He was describing an incident from his life which influenced his life very deeply.

"I became annoyed by the collision. Although the collision was not that strong, that it could have hurt me. But, I was angry, as the discipline of a renowned hospital was broken, by two youngsters." He further described.

Dr. Barnard was angry over both the children. This disturbance was made by two, not one child. Both of them were nearly thirteen years of age and admitted to the hospital as patients.

Dr. Barnard didn't recognize them, because, they were going treatment under other doctors.

But, they had broken the discipline of the hospital. Hence, Dr. Barnard was concerned.

He called both of them to his chamber, to get the explanation for the deed. After all this kind of activity disturbed the entire hospital and created an uneasy environment for other patients also. Being a patient doesn't mean that you are free to do anything.

They came to his chamber. But, after seeing those kids, his anger reduced to some extent; because, both of them were handicapped.

One was blind and the other one was disabled in both of his legs.

They did together the act (for which they were called up). The child who was blind was pushing the wheel chair and the other was sitting, shouting and guiding the path. So, they both were the culprits.

Now, the culprits were standing in front of Dr. Barnard. He observed both of them from top to bottom. They were wearing the uniform provided by the hospital to the admitted patients.

The face of the blind boy had scars as if he had been burned, and the other boy had both the legs disabled.

"So, what you both were doing? And, what do you want to prove by doing such kind of an activity? And, have you realized what you were doing?" Dr. Barnard asked, somewhat angrily.

"We want to live. We want to feel alive. That is all." They both answered in a single voice as if they were not two but one.

"What do you mean by this? Can you explain?" Dr. Barnard asked in an annoying tone.

"We had a bad accident, fifteen days before and from that time we are in this hospital. We both were living fantastic life, with our families." The blind one said.

The other was sitting silently, with sorrow in his eyes. His eyes were explaining the sorrow of their bad time, they were passing through.

"We were living as neighbors in a nearby village to this big city. We were and are very good friends." His eyes were glowing in the name of friendship.

He further explained.

"One day, we don't know how, a fire gripped the colony we were living in. The fire was so big that many flats burned immediately. In which our house burned together." Tears started flowing from eyes of both of them.

"Our families, nobody is alive now. Everyone from our family is dead. My father, mother; his father, mother and sister everyone is dead now." The flow of tears exceeded.

After a long pause, he again became able to explain further.

"I lost my both eyes, in that accident, due to burn on my face and my friend lost both his legs, as he jumped outside from the window and his spine got injured."

After pausing for some time more, he started telling again.

"Neighbors brought us here and admitted to this hospital. After some recovery we started talking, and consoling each other. Initially, we were very sad and living as if dead. But after getting each other's company, we started living our life again." A smile returned to both of them.

The other one explained with pride, looking at the face of the blind boy

"And, last night we have decided to show this world and to ourselves, that we are living, that we are alive and we can live our life with zest, with enthusiasm. And, to prove that, we have done what you have seen us doing."

And, they both started laughing; laughing as if to tell the whole world that they are happy.

Dr. Barnard was listening and a thought process rose up inside him. He had been angry but now he surprised by the courage these children showed. A soldier does not do a more courageous act during a time of war.

So, he leave them, but, made them understood that their enjoyment should not break the rules and discipline of the hospital.

But, something had changed, within Dr. Barnard.

"I am a well-known doctor of this country, a great utility for them but, am I really alive? Am I really living my life or have I just become a mechanical device, just a utility?"

He decided to take leave for some days after completing all his appointments, which meant visiting some remote hill station, where no one would know him.

He realized correctly that an incident of fire occurring in the life of these boys, had broken their identity with their old life. And, by and by those boys realized, that despite what they lost in their lives they can live, they can still live, still remain more alive.

So, Dr. Barnard took leave from his old patterns and decided to search for his real identity, which might be blissful.

He decided to go to a remote place, where nobody knew him, and to reflect upon whether he was thinking on the right track.

Reaching the destination and after spending some time he realized that he was right. Identifying much as Dr. Barnard he had lost his real identity and he was just working, working and working as a machine; just became a utility, nothing else.

..............*************...............

Try to understand this. This is a method, which I am giving you, and that can be used as a meditation technique.

Try to remain aware every moment, that you are not the name which society has given you, you are not the body or mind but you have to search for your real identity. Be aware of the fact. And, by and by your blissfulness will start increasing.

Swami Vivekananda says, that, remember you are loins thinking yourself as sheep. And it is true, your real identity is this vastness of the universe and you are thinking yourself as this name, this body.

And by saying this Swami Vivekananda is also trying to give you a meditation technique, over which I have tried to base this book.

Gurdjief's technique was also similar to this technique. The method he called 'self-remembrance'. He used this method in combination with his dynamic meditation techniques. He used this technique beautifully in the dance groups he had made. These groups were made up of his disciples who eventually were made to dance. When dance is at its peak, suddenly, he says stop and according to rule they have to stop in whatever position they were stopped.

He continued this pattern to dance again and stop. But, you have to understand how this is similar to what I am saying.

Imagine you are dancing; when you are really engaged in dancing only the dance remains, you cannot even remember yourself. If you're involved in dancing you cannot even remember your name and imagine, in that involvement, you have to stop suddenly in the position of dance you were in. For a moment you forget everything, your name, your society, your belongings, your possessions, your problems and suddenly bliss is possible.

In the moment you stop and your usual perception stops, and an identity different from your usual identity is possible and bliss happens. You fill up with bliss. Hence, Gurdjief's technique is very beautiful.

You can also try the method the way I have said. Just become aware every time that you are not your name, your body and your blissful nature will start to ignite itself in the light of your awareness. And, after starting, it will increase by and by. And, you become closer and closer to your real identity. And, your bliss will increase.

Try to become bliss not a utility.

Because, you are yourself, is bliss, not a utility.

THE CURTAIN

I named the previous chapter to make it clear that your name has different significances, when seen from different perspectives. For example, a society can use a name to make you a utility.

In this chapter I will emphasize that your name can be a hindrance in knowing your real nature, your real identity.

But, I want to make it clear that society cannot do anything different; it has to give you a name. When you think about society and why it is giving you a name, to recognize you or to make you a utility; whatever you think society is doing, it must give you a name.

Society cannot do anything about this but you can. That is the target of this book to make you aware that 'you can'. And, you can do it by igniting your awareness.

So, try this as a meditation and you will feel blissful.

Kabir Das, one of the most inspiring saints, has said, "Ghunghat ke pat khol re tohe pia milenge." Which in English means, that, open the curtain you are living in and then you will be able to see your lover, and that lover is none other than God himself.

So, you have to open that curtain; you have to renounce that curtain.

But, how can you renounce, you don't even know that you are living inside a curtain.

Have you ever realized the sort of life you are living and why are you living that kind of a life? Are you happy in that life, and if not happy why can't you change that life or the way you are living? But, that will be difficult for you to change. If I ask you; why? Why is it difficult? You will not be able to give a definite answer.

You cannot answer this question, because of a curtain, you are living behind. That curtain is preventing the light rays to come near you. How can you see without light? You are living in darkness, so how can you see?

Whatever perception you have, is given to you by society. Your liking, your disliking, even your feelings, are given to you by society. You think they are yours, but, these are given to you by society.

It is the result of the programming done to you by the society and by you, yourself.

And, this programming is the curtain, the curtain masking your real identity. Your real identity can only be that which you were born and you die with and which remains with you after death - that, which is constantly with you. And, knowing that is the bliss. But, for that, you have to drop the curtain, so that you can see the reality.

You are asleep now. You are asleep. You think yourself waking up in the morning. But, your waking is just partial.

You are not fully awakened. You are asleep, as you are; you are asleep.

I have heard a story of a disciple of Lao Tzu:

Lao Tzu was training one of his disciples in meditation. The disciple was kept in isolation, in a room, where all his basic needs were to be fulfilled. He was not allowed to meet anybody. Only meditation was permitted along with basic bodily requirements.

The meditation was to meant increase his inner awareness. After three months when Lao Tzu felt satisfied by the growth of his disciple who had attained the level of awareness or inner consciousness, Lao Tzu decided to allow that disciple to take a visit of the city along with him.

Both of them were visiting the city. They visited the market, they visited residential places.

"How are you feeling"? Lao Tzu asked while visiting the city.

"Everything is alright but I am feeling strange, when I look at humans." the disciple said.

"What strange they are"? Asked Lao Tzu

"When I look at them I sense that they are asleep. My feeling is they are doing everything as if while asleep, as if in their dreams. The shopkeeper is selling goods while sleeping; people are buying as if asleep", explained the disciple...

"What has happened to the world in these three months? How have they are changed so much?" asked the disciple.

Lao Tzu said, "Nothing has happened to the world. But, something has happened to you. You have awakened your consciousness in these three months. You have arisen out of your sleep, and the world has remained sleeping as usual".

Could this be true, we all are living as if living in a deep sleep? When you say that you have arisen, consciousness is just relative. That means while sleeping you are fully unconscious but while you have awakened you are partially conscious, not fully conscious. You can watch this. Sometimes while reading a book, you must have felt that you have read a full page, but not able to remember a single word from that page.

What happened? If, you were fully conscious, then, where have you missed the words or page? We are asleep. We are asleep as we are; as if living in hypnosis and this is because of the programing done to us by society and by ourselves.

Meditation is a way through which you can get out of this hypnosis, this sleep, this programming.

And remember your name is the biggest tool through which this hypnosis is possible. Society cannot program you without your name.

But, you can be out of this hypnosis with the help of meditation. Choose any type of meditation, whether the technique I have already discussed in this book or some other you like. But, add some sort meditation in your life.

……………*************……………

I have another anecdote to tell:

Out of love towards his master a disciple, one day, offered his master to build a house; as his master didn't have one. So, he offered to build a house for his master at a chosen property. He wanted his master to live in a house built by him. Perhaps he thought he was offering this house building from innate love. But I tell you this was the subtle way in which proud is going to make abode in the disciple's heart, that, he is doing a great sacrifice for his master.

So, he offered to build.

His master accepted and allowed him to proceed further.

After some months he completed the work. The house made was beautiful. He was very excited to gift it to his master. After all the details refurbished to his satisfaction he rushed to show it to his master.

Master came to see the house. After touring the house with interest and admiration, he surprisingly ordered the disciple to demolish the house and construct it once more.

He was surprised and disappointed, but his master has ordered, so, he couldn't disobey. He demolished it. The house was quite strong, so, even demolishing took great effort. After demolishing he again started to build it up.

After months of hard work again, a beautiful house was ready to be shown. He was again very excited and this time the house was so good and so well equipped with every sort of a luxury, and he was sure that this time his master would accept it. He was more excited and confident.

So he went to the master and asked him to please see the house as his gift and accept it. Master came again and after seeing and admiring the whole house, to his surprise again the master ordered to demolish it and construct another one at the same place. The disciple was puzzled, why his house had not been accepted and why his master has admired if he didn't wanted to accept it.

But, for him the order of his master was of supreme importance. He had trust over his master, which could not be broken.

So, he again started the work. Demolished and reconstructed but more beautifully. Again he rushed to build with more confidence to call his master. But, master rejected again after appreciation.

Doing like this years passed away but he constructed and his master rejected.

Twenty five years passed away like this. And, this is again time for him to show a new house to his master. This time master came and saw the whole house.

He asked his disciple, "Can you remember how many times you constructed the house and according to my instructions demolished it."

"I have done this work so many times that I even don't remember the number of times I have done this."

"That is my message to you my child." The master said lovingly.

"For so many lives you are doing this building house, making families, getting married. In this same life you wanted to gift me with a house. You want to get associated with me. My purpose is for you realize this fact that you are not this name or body or your mind. You are something else. Identify yourself. Do not waste your life in making houses. Realize the fact that houses are destructible. This house making is only repetition, as you have repeated as per my orders. Now know yourself."

It is said that after these words by the master, he realized himself, he became enlightened.

That constructing the house and demolishing became a meditation for him and he became realized. He identified himself.

..........***********.........

That is also true for you. Your name is not your real identity. Instead your name is the hindrance, in knowing the fact, because you get identified with your name. Awareness, a continuous remembrance is needed to know that you are not your name or body.

To understand the way you are programmed, I have another anecdote to tell:

This anecdote is from the life of Ashtawakra, who was a significant figure in the world of spirituality. He had written outstanding books, in which, Ashtawakra Gita was most important.

Ashtawakra was the son of a servant working under king Janak. He belonged to a family caste which was thought to be of low caste at that time.

Caste system was very prevalent at that time in India. People were divided into lower cast and upper cast. Those of lower caste were treated as untouchable by people of upper cast. But, Ashtawakra was a very intelligent person; a brilliant scholar; no other person at that time was of his stature.

But, Ashtawakra had two drawbacks in his life. One was that he belonged to a low caste family and the other, that his body was bent at eight places, so, he looked palsied and an object of derision for everyone.

That was an introduction of Ashtawakra.

Now the anecdote:

King Janak was a great scholar himself and remained interested in discussing philosophy and spirituality.

So, he called upon all the scholars from his state and surrounding states for a meeting in which they can gather for a discussion on the subject of philosophy and spirituality.

Great scholars arrived. But, Ashtawakra was not invited. How could he be invited, after all he belonged to low caste and was the son of a servant?

The palace was full of scholars from all over the world. King Janak was seated and ready to start the discussion.

Ashtawakra also didn't want to go to the palace where the meeting was going on. He was not invited after all. But, he was called upon to substitute for his father's job, which was ill on that day; Ashtawakra was to go against his own wishes.

He reached inside the palace and walked limping towards the king. Laughter of all the scholars was surrounded him. All were derisive, on seeing his body and the way he was walking.

Ashtawakra didn't say anything but when the laughter continues he answered the laughter with laughter. He started laughing loudly. Whole of the palace echoed with his laughter. After listening to this type of laughter everyone stopped laughing.

Ashtawakra said angrily, to the king, "Why are you wasting your time with these fools. You called this meeting in the hope of gaining some knowledge, but, I tell you, you are wasting your time. These people cannot be scholars; these people are the businessmen who sell skins. They are the knowers of the skin, not of the philosophy, not of the spirituality. They are buyer and sellers of flesh. They are the knowers of flesh and skin. That is why they are laughing at me and my body, assessing me by my skin."

Janak immediately realized the truth, how could a scholar of philosophy or spirituality laugh at a disabled person. Janak immediately ended the meeting. Saying sorry to Ashtawakra he requested him to say something about spirituality.

…………..*********………
…

But, here I have mentioned this anecdote to make you understand that even scholars could have blurred visions, if they are living according to the programming given by the society.

As in this story, society says that low caste people cannot produce a great scholar but, Ashtawakra was a great scholar belonging to a low caste. And the scholars who are looking from behind the curtain given by society didn't recognize the great scholar behind a disabled body and a low caste.

So, the programming, the hypnosis, done to you by society and by yourself make your vision blurred and you then become unable to see the reality, the truth.

Even your real identity is different from that which you have thought to be so far.

You are something different from what you think yourself to be.

You are not your name.

You are not your body.

You are not your thoughts.

You are not your mind.

You are not your shadow.

So stop running after your shadow.

Make it a meditation.

Make truth itself your meditation.

Meditate upon the fact; that you are not your name.

Renounce the curtain of your name.

And you will be close to your reality.

You will be close to your real identity.

THE BEYOND

So far, we have discussed that how your name is a utility to the society and to you and also discussed how it helps in the programming or how it is used as a programming tool.

But, in this chapter we will try to emphasize your real identity, which is beyond your name or your body.

Have you ever thought of this? What would happen if there were no mirrors in this world or you would not have any instrument to see your face? Then is it possible to imagine your own face? Then would you have any face for yourself? You could imagine your face but never see it. In that condition you cannot have any face.

Try to understand this. In that condition you have to search for your real face, because, you don't have any instrument to see it directly.

You need an instrument to see, even your physical identity. Without the instrument, it is nearly impossible.

Remember, even for seeing physical identity, you need an instrument - then, what about your real or spiritual identity.

For that also you need instruments.

For a physical identity you need physical instrument.

What about spiritual identity?

Definitely you will need an instrument from a different dimension.

You will need an instrument that can develop an eye to see the beyond.

You will need an instrument which can make you aware so that you can see that you are different from the identity you got in this world.

You need an instrument that can connect you from the beyond.

You are the beyond; Beyond everything; which, you can see or can imagine.

Upanishads says neti neti. That means you are not this, you are not that.

You are the beyond.

I have heard:

A disciple went to his master and asked, "Dear master! What is my real identity? I want to know."

The master said, "Go and search within."

He went and came back after three months to his master and said, "I have searched within. So far I have searched that I am not the body."

The master said, “Okay! You have found this much, which is a big achievement, but, go and search further within".

He came back after three months and told his master, "I now know the fact that I am also not my thoughts. I am not my mind".

The master said, "Okay! Even this much is a great achievement and now you are not very distant from the fact. So, go and search further".

He returned after three years. But this time he returned dancing as if he found some treasure.

"Master now I have known it but I don't have words to tell you. I can just say that I am the beyond".

Master said, "No need to tell. Your whole gesture is showing that you have known the truth".

Remember, his last words 'I am the beyond'.

‘You are the beyond!’

Beyond everything that you can see or imagine.

But to see that beyond, you need an instrument and that instrument is 'Meditation'.

Try some meditation technique.

The technique I have discussed in this book or any other technique.

But try some meditation to know the truth.

And the truth is that you are the beyond…..

Beyond your name…..

Beyond your body…..

Beyond your mind……

Beyond everything……..

'You are the beyond.'